Written by
Maureen Boylan and Traci Geiser

Editors: LaDawn Walter and Kim Cernek
Illustrator: Mark Mason
Cover Illustrator: David Willardson
Designer/Production: Moonhee Pak/Carrie Carter
Cover Designer: Moonhee Pak
Art Director: Tom Cochrane
Project Director: Carolea Williams

Table of Contents

Introduction

Save valuable instruction time when you implement theme-based mini-units that combine science content with literacy lessons. The resources in *Leap into Literacy* are designed to creatively meet national science and language standards for preK through first-grade students.

The dynamic activities in *Leap into Literacy* directly complement your regular language arts instruction block—freeing more time in your daily schedule. And, this resource gives emergent readers the frequent, repetitive, and intensive opportunities they need to practice the literacy skills of reading, writing, listening, and speaking while they acquire new science knowledge.

Each of the eight fall-related units includes a science-based song and poem; two student mini-books that use the same text as the song and poem; related science facts; literature links; a class book activity; a home–school reading connection; and a variety of center activities. Each mini-book and center activity addresses the standards of a comprehensive science and literacy program (see page 4).

Leap into Literacy provides everything you need to maximize your instruction time: simple directions, a wealth of reproducibles (including mini-book pages, word and letter cards, manipulatives, puzzles), and activities that are quick and easy to prepare. With a variety of fun, hands-on, language-based activities, children are sure to love learning about science as they leap into literacy!

Standards Connections

One of the goals of *Leap into Literacy* is to provide you with activities that combine the standards of authentic science and literacy instruction. The activities give children practice with the following skills:

Practice reading readiness skills that include
- front-to-back orientation
- left-to-right orientation
- top-to-bottom orientation
- one-to-one correspondence

Explore language use and patterns by
- matching uppercase and lowercase letters
- identifying consonant digraphs
- recognizing sight words (including color and number words)
- identifying beginning, middle, and ending sounds
- demonstrating alphabetical order
- identifying word families
- matching short-vowel sounds
- discriminating between singular and plural words
- recognizing prepositions
- identifying the number of syllables in a word
- blending phonemes
- rhyming

Experience literature by
- memorizing theme-based, rhyming mini-books
- listening to and reading fiction and nonfiction trade books
- sequencing a story
- writing a personal response to a story
- maintaining a reading log

Investigate science content that teaches the properties of
- life science, including plants and animals
- health and nutrition

Practice other basic skills that include
- matching opposites
- following directions
- developing fine motor skills

Unit Components

Leap into Literacy

Use the following reading readiness activities to introduce the unit's science topic and to capture children's attention and interest. These activities encourage children to practice their literacy skills (i.e., reading, writing, speaking, and listening) and learn and experience new science concepts.

Songs and Poems

Each unit opens with a thematic song and poem. Sing these cute and clever verses to familiar children's tunes and read or chant them during circle time and/or transition time to help build oral language skills and introduce and reinforce science concepts. Copy the song and poem onto an overhead transparency and cut them apart to present them separately, or use a different colored marker to write each line of the song and poem on a large piece of chart paper or sentence strips. Display the overhead transparency or chart paper, or place the sentence strips in a pocket chart. (If you use sentence strips, color the pictures from the mini-books, cut them out, and place each picture next to the corresponding sentence strip.) Read aloud each line of the song and poem, and have children repeat the lines.

Then, sing each line of the song to its familiar tune, and invite children to repeat each line using their "singing voices." Once children are familiar with the words to the song and poem, they will be ready to read the corresponding mini-books.

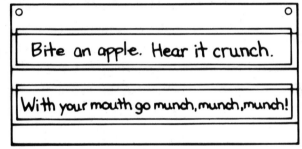

Mini-Books

Children have likely already memorized the fun, rhyming text from the readiness activities, so you can use the mini-books to give them interactive practice with book-reading skills, including reading front-to-back, left-to-right, and top-to-bottom, as they learn scientific ideas. The first mini-book in each unit is written in simple verse and uses the same text as the unit's song. The second mini-book offers additional science information and uses the same text as the unit's poem.

For each unit, prepare a class set of the two mini-books. Copy a one-sided set of the mini-book pages for each child. Cut the pages in half, place them in numerical order, and staple them together on the left-hand side. Use the activity ideas on page 6 to help familiarize children with the words for each mini-book. Then, use the mini-books for whole-group or small-group reading instruction. Have children color-code or circle key words or phrases. Ask them to write their name on the first page. Read aloud with children the sentences on each page. Invite them to color the illustrations after they read the book. Encourage children to reread the book with a partner and take it home for extra practice.

Extensions

Use these activity ideas throughout the unit to give children additional practice reading the poem and singing the song.

- Use decorated "magic wands" or theme-related reading sticks to point to the words as children sing or read.
- Tape-record the class singing or reading. Place copies of the song sheet or poem and the cassette at a listening center for children to use.
- Create hand and body movements to accompany the words of the song or poem, and encourage children to use them as they sing or read.
- Invite children to use simple instruments or jump ropes as they sing.
- Ask a volunteer to point to each word on the song or poem chart.
- Invite children to sing a solo or duet in front of the class.
- Write the song or poem on sentence strips. Distribute the sentence strips to volunteers. While the class sings, have volunteers place their strip in the appropriate place in a pocket chart.
- Give each child a copy of the song or poem. Have children underline any high-frequency or sight words that you are working on in class.
- Give each child a three-ring binder. Have children put a copy of each song and poem in their binder. Encourage them to reread the songs and poems in class. Invite children to take home their binder at the end of the school year for continued reading practice.

Find Out the Facts

Each unit features a page of facts about the science topic. Use this information and the following ideas to introduce each unit and to help build and extend children's background science knowledge.

KWL Charts

At the beginning of each unit, create a KWL chart. Draw three columns on a large piece of chart paper or butcher paper. Label the columns *What We **K**now*, *What We **W**ant to Know*, and *What We **L**earned*. Fill in the first two columns before the unit begins and the last column at the end of each unit.

Murals

Have children create murals that feature the science facts. Copy the fun facts page, cut apart the fact strips, and read aloud and discuss the meaning of each fact with children. Give each pair of children a 12" x 18" (30.5 cm x 46 cm) piece of construction paper and a fact strip. Ask children to glue their fact strip at the bottom of their paper and illustrate it at the top. Invite children to present their fact to the class, and then display the papers around the room.

Bounce into Books

Use theme-related picture books to introduce and extend the information in the unit. Place the books in a class library, or arrange for children to take them home to read.

Literature Links

Each unit includes a list of fiction and nonfiction titles. Select a variety of books from the list. Read these books to children to help generate and retain their interest in the unit's theme, to model reading skills, and to build background science knowledge.

Reading Logs

Copy the reading log reproducible for the unit. Tell children to color one picture for each book about the theme (including mini-books) they read at home. Send home the reading log and the parent letter (page 8) at the beginning of each unit. At the end of each unit, invite children to bring their completed reading log back to school to receive a reward. (Use special certificates, or give children decorated reading sticks, stickers, erasers, pencils, or bookmarks.)

Class Books

Create science-based class books to provide children with writing experiences and fine motor skill development. Read aloud several books from the literature links list and share the facts from the unit's fun facts page before you create the class books. Copy the class book reproducible, and invite children to complete the frame and illustrate the page as directed. Write the title of the unit (e.g., *Apples*) on a construction paper cover, bind together the children's completed pages, and read the book aloud during circle time. Place the class book in your classroom library, or send it home for children and parents to read.

Spring into Centers

Use the developmentally appropriate, hands-on center activities that incorporate thematic science concepts to extend children's learning of literacy and language arts skills (e.g., rhyming, blending words, identifying consonant digraphs, recognizing uppercase and lowercase letters, forming sentences) and science knowledge. Copy the reproducibles, cut out the pieces, laminate them for durability, and place them in a folder or plastic container for easy access. These activities are designed for two to three children to complete during small-group time or free time or as extra independent practice when children have completed their regular assignments and activities.

Parent Letter

Dear Parents,

We will soon begin another exciting science unit called

We will learn a song and poem about this topic. The words to this song and poem also appear in the mini-books that we will take home to practice reading.

Please read the mini-books and other books that are related to our science topic to and with your child. After your child listens to or reads a book, ask him or her to color one of the pictures at the bottom of the attached reading log. Have your child return his or her reading log when all five pictures are colored and he or she will receive a special reward.

Enjoy yourselves because learning about science while you practice reading is really a lot of fun!

Leap into Literacy • Fall © 2003 Creative Teaching Press

Apple Treats

(to the tune of "Old MacDonald Had a Farm")

What can you make with apples?
Foods that are so sweet.
Get ready and soon you'll have
Lots of things to eat.

Like some apple pie,
And applesauce,
Apple butter,
Apple bread,
Apple juice, and cider.

What can you make with apples?
Many yummy treats!

Apples

An apple is a fruit that grows on a tree.
Pick one for you. Pick one for me.

See the shape—small and round.
Shake it. It does not make a sound.

Smell it. It's so fresh and sweet.
Yummy, yummy, what a treat!

Bite an apple. Hear it crunch.
With your mouth go munch, munch, munch!

Apple Treats

by _____

What can you make with apples?
Foods that are so sweet.

Get ready and soon you'll have
lots of things to eat.

2

Like some apple pie,
and applesauce,

3

apple butter, apple bread,

4

apple juice, and cider.

5

What can you make with apples?

6

Many yummy treats!

7

Apples

by _____

An apple is a fruit that grows on a tree.
Pick one for you. Pick one for me.

Leap into Literacy • Fall © 2003 Creative Teaching Press

See the shape—small and round.

2

Shake it. It does not make a sound.
Smell it. It's so fresh and sweet.

Yummy, yummy, what a treat!

4

Bite an apple. Hear it crunch.
With your mouth go munch, munch, munch!

5

Leap into Literacy • Fall © 2003 Creative Teaching Press

Find Out the Facts

Apples

ACTIVITIES

Use the fun facts reproducible on page 20 and the activity suggestions on page 6 to introduce children to new vocabulary and extend their science knowledge.

Bounce into Books

Literature Links

Fiction

The Apple Pie Tree
by Zoe Hall
(SCHOLASTIC)

Down the Road
by Alice Schertle
(HARCOURT)

Johnny Appleseed
by Steven Kellogg
(WILLIAM MORROW & COMPANY)

The Seasons of Arnold's Apple Tree
by Gail Gibbons
(HARCOURT)

Ten Red Apples
by Pat Hutchins
(GREENWILLOW BOOKS)

Nonfiction

Apples
by Gail Gibbons
(HOLIDAY HOUSE)

Apples
by Rhoda Nottridge
(CAROLRHODA BOOKS)

Apples, How They Grow
by Bruce McMillan
(HOUGHTON MIFFLIN)

How Do Apples Grow?
by Betsy Maestro
(HARPERCOLLINS)

Picking Apples
by Gail Saunders-Smith
(CAPSTONE)

Reading Log

Use the reproducible on page 21 as a reading log (see page 7).

Class Book

- Copy the class book reproducible (page 22) for children to complete.
- Have children draw what they would make if they had a basket of apples.

Spring into Centers

Apple Fun

Skills: recognizing basic sight words and visual discrimination

Materials

Apples reproducible (page 23)

newspapers and magazines

glue sticks

scissors

Apples Copy the Apples reproducible, and write on each apple a sight word, such as *and, the,* and *to.* Give each child a copy of the revised paper, newspapers, magazines, and a glue stick. Review each sight word with children several times. Invite children to look for the sight words in the newspapers and magazines. When children find any of these words, have them cut out the words and glue their cutouts on the apple above that word. To extend the activity, use different sight or vocabulary words.

Apple Pickin'

Skill: discriminating between long and short vowels

Copy and color the Basket and Tree reproducibles, and laminate them. Make two copies of the Apples reproducible, and cut out the apples. Write *apple, alligator, ant, cap, bag, basket, ran, sand, cane, late, make,* and *tape* on separate apples, and color and laminate them. Have children place the basket and tree faceup on a flat surface and place all of the apples on the tree. Explain to children that the /a/ in *basket* is short and that the /a/ in *cane* is long. Invite children to place the apples that have the same /a/ as in *basket* in the basket and leave the other apples in the tree. Ask children to read aloud the short *a* and long *a* words.

Materials

Basket reproducible
(page 24)

Tree reproducible (page 25)

Apples reproducible (page 23)

crayons or markers

scissors

Wiggly Apple Worms

Skills: matching uppercase and lowercase letters and alphabetical order

Materials

Apples reproducible (page 23)

Worms reproducible
(page 26)

scissors

Make five copies of the Apples and Worms reproducibles, and cut apart the apples and worms. Write an uppercase *A* on an apple and a lowercase *a* on a worm. Repeat with uppercase and lowercase letters for B–Z, and laminate the pieces. Have children place the pieces on a flat surface in alphabetical order. Then, have them place each worm on the apple with the matching uppercase letter. To simplify the activity, do not have children alphabetize the letters first. Have them instead match the uppercase and lowercase letters. To extend the activity, write onsets and rhymes on the apples and worms, and have children match them.

Apple Fun Facts

There are more apple trees in the world than any other kind of tree. There are more than 7,500 kinds of apples.

An apple tree begins to grow apples when it is five to seven years old.

The leaves on an apple tree make a certain kind of sugar that feeds the apples and makes them grow.

The middle of an apple is called the core.

The core has five seed chambers. They are little open pockets that hold two seeds.

Most of an apple is water, but it is also vitamins, minerals, sugar, and fiber.

Reading Log

Name _____   Date _____

My favorite book about **apples** was

_____

because _____

_____.

Color one book each time you read or listen to a story about apples.

Leap into Literacy • Fall © 2003 Creative Teaching Press

Name _____ Date _____

If I had a basket of apples,

I would make_____

_____.

Leap into Literacy • Fall © 2003 Creative Teaching Press

Apples

Basket

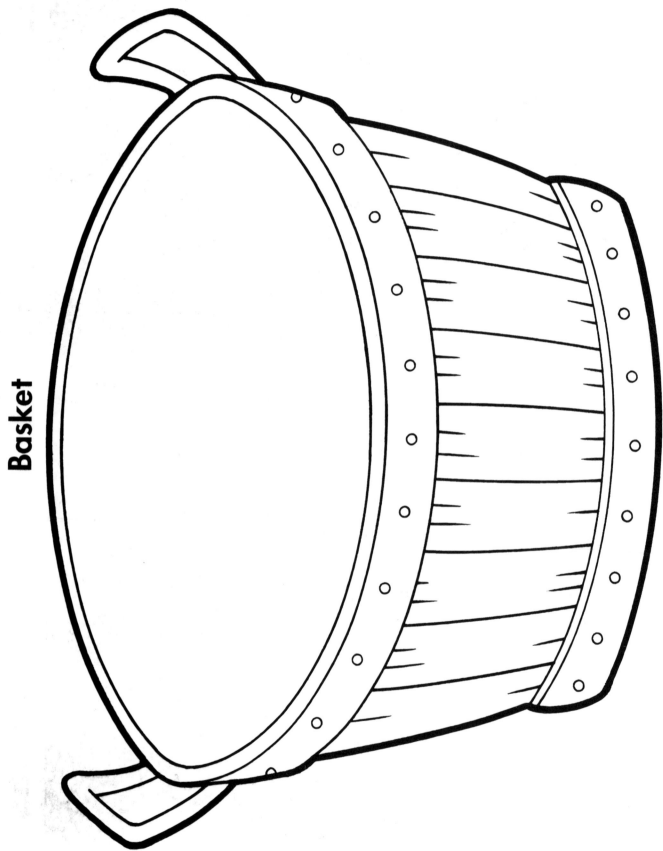

Leap into Literacy • Fall © 2003 Creative Teaching Press

Tree

Worms

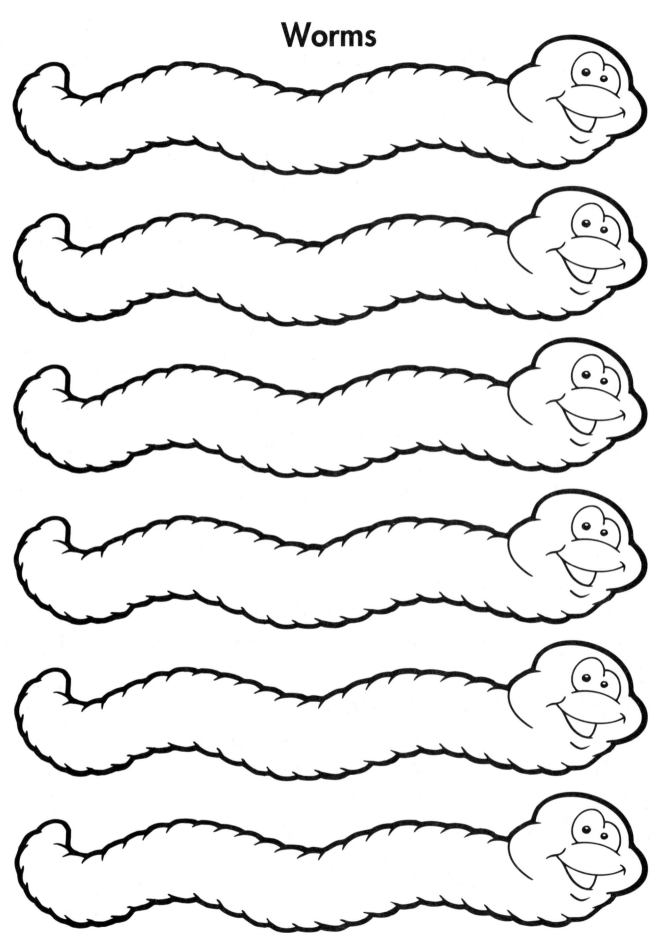

Leap into Literacy • Fall © 2003 Creative Teaching Press

Healthy Habits

(to the tune of "Row, Row, Row Your Boat")

Brush, brush, brush your teeth.
Get them nice and clean.
Don't forget to use some floss
To clean them in between.

Take, take, take a bath.
Scrub from head to toe.
Fingers, toes, behind your ears—
You're looking good you know!

Drink, drink, drink some water.
Your body needs a lot.
Four to eight glasses a day—
Especially when it's hot!

Get lots of exercise,
But don't forget to rest.
Exercise and lots of sleep
Will help you feel your best!

Staying Healthy

Brush your teeth, and floss them, too.
Taking a bath is a good thing to do.
Exercise every day.
Wash your hands to keep germs away.
Get lots of sleep. Eat food that's good.
And you'll stay as healthy as you should!

Healthy Habits

by _____

Brush, brush, brush your teeth.
Get them nice and clean.

Leap into Literacy • Fall © 2003 Creative Teaching Press

Don't forget to use some floss
to clean them in between.

2

Take, take, take a bath.
Scrub from head to toe.

3

Fingers, toes, behind your ears—
you're looking good you know!

4

Drink, drink, drink some water.
Your body needs a lot.

5

Four to eight glasses a day—
especially when it's hot!

6

Get lots of exercise,
but don't forget to rest.

7

Leap into Literacy • Fall © 2003 Creative Teaching Press

Exercise and lots of sleep

8

will help you feel your best!

9

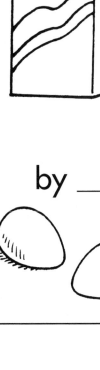

Staying Healthy

by _____

Brush your teeth, and floss them, too.
Taking a bath is a good thing to do.

1

Exercise every day.

2

Wash your hands to keep germs away.

Leap into Literacy • Fall © 2003 Creative Teaching Press

Get lots of sleep. Eat food that's good.

4

And you'll stay as healthy as you should!

5

Leap into Literacy • Fall © 2003 Creative Teaching Press

Health and Nutrition

ACTIVITIES

Find Out the Facts

Use the fun facts reproducible on page 39 and the activity suggestions on page 6 to introduce children to new vocabulary and extend their science knowledge.

Bounce into Books

Literature Links

Fiction

I Know Why I Brush My Teeth
by Kate Rowan
(CANDLEWICK PRESS)

Mr. Sugar Came to Town
adapted by Harriet Rohmer
and Cruz Gomez
(CHILDREN'S BOOK PRESS)

Ms. Sneed's Guide to Hygiene
by Dale Gottlieb
(CHRONICLE BOOKS)

Wash, Scrub, Brush!
by Mick Manning and Brita Granstrom
(ALBERT WHITMAN)

Who's Sick Today?
by Lynne Cherry
(DUTTON)

Nonfiction

Eating Right
by Helen Frost
(PEBBLE BOOKS)

Food Rules
by Bill Haduch
(DUTTON)

Good Enough to Eat: A Kids Guide to Food and Nutrition
by Lizzy Rockwell
(HARPERCOLLINS)

Hygiene and Your Health
by Jillian Powell
(RAINTREE STECK-VAUGHN PUBLISHERS)

I'm Happy, I'm Healthy
by Alexandra Parsons
(FRANKLIN WATTS)

Reading Log

Use the reproducible on page 40 as a reading log (see page 7).

Class Book

- Copy the class book reproducible (page 41) for children to complete.
- Have children think of different types of food and write about them.

Appetizing Alphabet

Skills: arranging in alphabetical order and identifying beginning sounds

Health and Nutrition

Make four copies of the Plates reproducible. Write the alphabet from A to Z (omitting Q and X) on separate plates. Color and cut apart the plates, and laminate them. Copy and color the Food Cards, cut them apart, and laminate them. Have children arrange the plates in alphabetical order. (Be sure to tell them that Q and X are missing.) Ask children to pick a food card and say the name of the food on it. Repeat the beginning sound of the word with children. Have them tell you what letter makes that sound. Invite children to find the plate that has that letter and place the card on the plate. To simplify the activity, alphabetize the plates for children.

Materials

Plates reproducible (page 42)

Food Cards (pages 43–44)

crayons or markers

scissors

Food Fun

Skill: rhyming words

Materials

Rhyming Cards (page 45)

scissors

writing paper

Health and Nutrition

Copy and cut apart the Rhyming Cards. Have children place the cards faceup on a flat surface. Encourage children to examine the picture on each card, and help them read aloud each word. Invite children to pick a card, read the word on it, and find another card with a rhyming word. When children have all the cards, encourage them to write the rhyming words on a piece of paper. To simplify the activity, have children match the cards but not write the words.

Healthy Habits

Skill: sequencing

Materials

Sequence Cards (page 46)

scissors

Health and Nutrition

Copy and cut apart the Sequence Cards. Write *a, b,* or *c* on the back of each set of related cards to show their sequence. Have children pick a set of three cards, and ask them to examine the picture on each card. Tell children to put the cards in order from left to right. Have them turn over the three cards to check their work. Have children repeat these steps with the other three sets of cards.

Health and Nutrition Fun Facts

We should eat 6–11 servings of grains a day. Some grains are wheat bread, cereal, and pasta.

We should eat 3–5 servings of vegetables a day. Some vegetables are carrots, broccoli, and corn.

We should eat 2–4 servings of fruits a day. Some fruits are grapes, strawberries, and apples.

We should eat 2–3 servings of meat and protein a day. Some of these foods are chicken, nuts, and fish.

We should eat 2–4 servings of milk and/or milk products. Some of these foods are cheese and yogurt.

Our bodies are made mostly of water. It is very important to drink 4 to 8 glasses of water each day.

Reading Log

Name _____ Date _____

My favorite book about **health and nutrition**

was_____

because _____

_____ .

Color one book each time you read or listen to a story about health and nutrition.

Name _____ Date _____

My favorite grain is _____.

My favorite fruit is _____.

My favorite vegetable is _____.

My favorite meat and/or protein is _____.

My favorite special sweet treat is _____.

Leap into Literacy • Fall © 2003 Creative Teaching Press

Plates

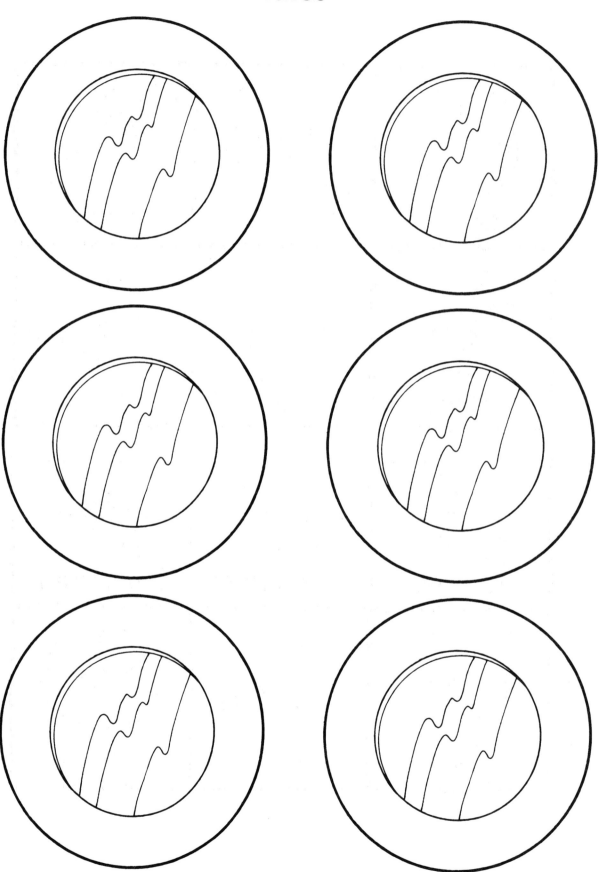

Leap into Literacy • Fall © 2003 Creative Teaching Press

Food Cards

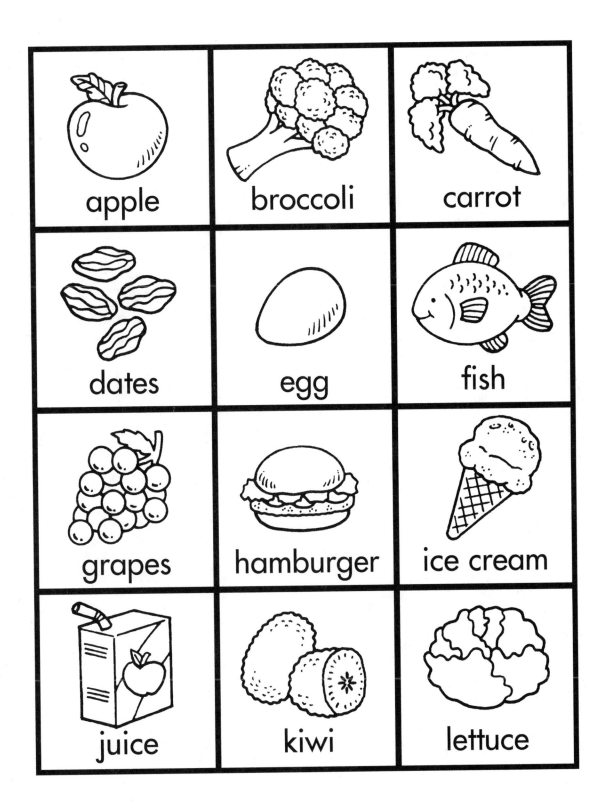

apple

broccoli

carrot

dates

egg

fish

grapes

hamburger

ice cream

juice

kiwi

lettuce

Food Cards

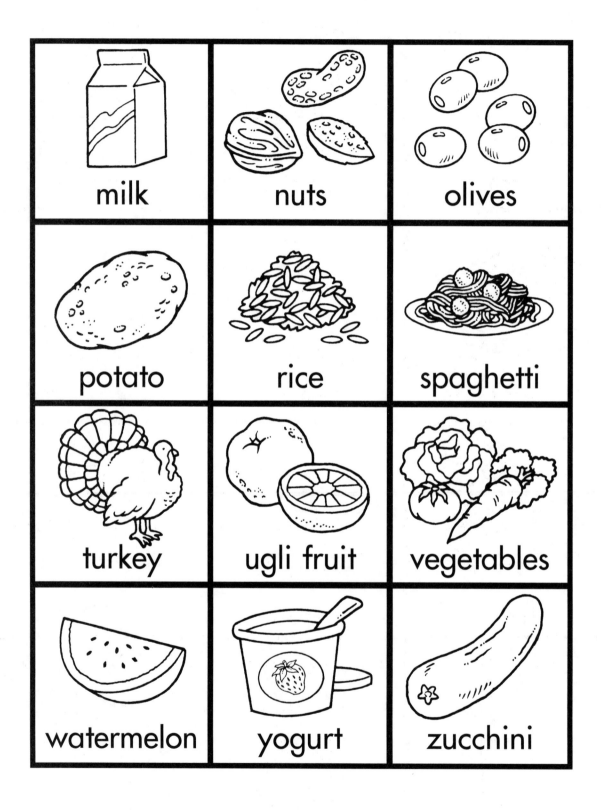

milk

nuts

olives

potato

rice

spaghetti

turkey

ugli fruit

vegetables

watermelon

yogurt

zucchini

Leap into Literacy • Fall © 2003 Creative Teaching Press

Rhyming Cards

yam	ham	cherry
strawberry	potato	tomato
fish	dish	rice
spice	can	pan

Sequence Cards

Leap into Literacy • Fall © 2003 Creative Teaching Press

Night Owls

(to the tune of "The Alphabet Song")

Nocturnal animals sleep all day.
And at night they work and play.
Bush babies and field mice are up at night.
Owls and bats do not like the light.
One of these animals might surprise you
If at night you're awake, too!

While You Are Asleep

A nocturnal animal will creep
While you are asleep.

Owl and raccoon
Hunt by the moon.

Scorpion and snake
At night are awake.

Field mouse and bat—
The dark—they like that.

While you are asleep,
A nocturnal animal will creep.

Night Owls

by _____

Nocturnal animals sleep all day.
And at night they work and play.

Leap into Literacy • Fall © 2003 Creative Teaching Press

Bush babies and field mice are up at night.

2

Owls and bats do not like the light.

3

One of these animals might surprise you

4

if at night you're awake, too!

Leap into Literacy • Fall © 2003 Creative Teaching Press

While You Are Asleep

by _____

A nocturnal animal will creep
while you are asleep.

1

Owl and raccoon
hunt by the moon.

2

Scorpion and snake
at night are awake.

3

Leap into Literacy • Fall © 2003 Creative Teaching Press

Field mouse and bat—
the dark—they like that.

4

While you are asleep,
a nocturnal animal will creep.

5

Nocturnal Animals

ACTIVITIES

Find Out the Facts

Use the fun facts reproducible on page 57 and the activity suggestions on page 6 to introduce children to new vocabulary and extend their science knowledge.

Bounce into Books

Literature Links

Fiction

Desert Song
by Tony Johnston
(SIERRA CLUB BOOKS FOR CHILDREN)

The Kissing Hand
by Audrey Penn
(CHILD WELFARE LEAGUE OF AMERICA)

Oliver's Wood
by Sue Hendra
(CANDLEWICK PRESS)

Owl Babies
by Martin Waddell
(CANDLEWICK PRESS)

Wake-Up Kisses
by Pamela Duncan Edwards
and Henry Cole
(HARPERCOLLINS)

Nonfiction

The Giant Book of Night Creatures
by Jim Pipe
(COPPER BEECH BOOKS)

The Night Book
by Pamela Hickman
(KIDS CAN PRESS)

Night Creatures
created by Gallimard Jeunesse
(CARTWHEEL BOOKS®)

Night-Time Animals
by Angela Royston
(ALADDIN)

Where Are the Night Animals?
by Mary Ann Fraser
(HARPERCOLLINS)

Reading Log

Use the reproducible on page 58 as a reading log (see page 7).

Class Book

- Copy the class book reproducible (page 59) for children to complete.
- Have children draw a nocturnal animal and write why they like it.

Critter Count

Skill: counting syllables

Nocturnal Animals Make three copies of the Night reproducible, and number them from 1 to 3. Color and laminate the papers. Copy, color, and cut apart the Animal Cards, and laminate them. Have children place the three night papers in numerical order and the animal cards faceup on a flat surface. Ask children to choose a card and say the name of the animal. Invite children to sound out the word and clap the syllables at the same time. Invite them to name the number of syllables in the word and place the card on the mat with the corresponding number. To simplify the activity, only give children words with one or two syllables.

Materials

Night reproducible (page 60)

Animal Cards (page 61)

crayons or markers

scissors

Batty Blending

Skill: blending phonemes

Materials

Bats reproducible (page 62)

Cave reproducibles
(pages 63–64)

scissors

crayons or markers

writing paper

 Nocturnal Animals

Make two copies of the Bats reproducible, and cut them apart. Write *b, br, c, d, l, m, n, p, r, s, sh,* and *w* on separate bats, and laminate them. Copy, color, and laminate the Cave reproducibles. Have children place a bat in the box in each of the four caves. Invite them to blend the sounds on the bat and the cave to make words. Ask children to write real words on a piece of paper. Encourage children to change the bats to make new real words.

Animal Action

Skills: following directions and identifying verbs

Materials

Direction Cards (page 65)

crayons or markers

scissors

 Nocturnal Animals

Copy, color, cut apart, and laminte the Direction Cards. Have children pick a card, and help them read aloud the direction. Ask children to act out the directions on the card.

Nocturnal Animal Fun Facts

Nocturnal animals sleep during the day and are awake at night.

Many snakes have a good sense of vibration. This helps them sense other animals that are close.

Bats use high-pitched noises that echo back to them to find their way through the dark at night.

Many owls have very soft feathers that allow them to fly silently and sneak up on their prey in the dark.

Panthers hide well in the dark because they are black. They have a strong sense of smell to help them catch their prey.

Scorpions hide under the sand in the desert. They catch insects with their claws and sting them with their tail.

Reading Log

Name _____ Date _____

My favorite book about **nocturnal animals** was

_____

because _____

_____.

Color one book each time you read or listen to a story about nocturnal animals.

Leap into Literacy • Fall © 2003 Creative Teaching Press

Name _____   Date _____

 I like _____

the best because they are

_____.

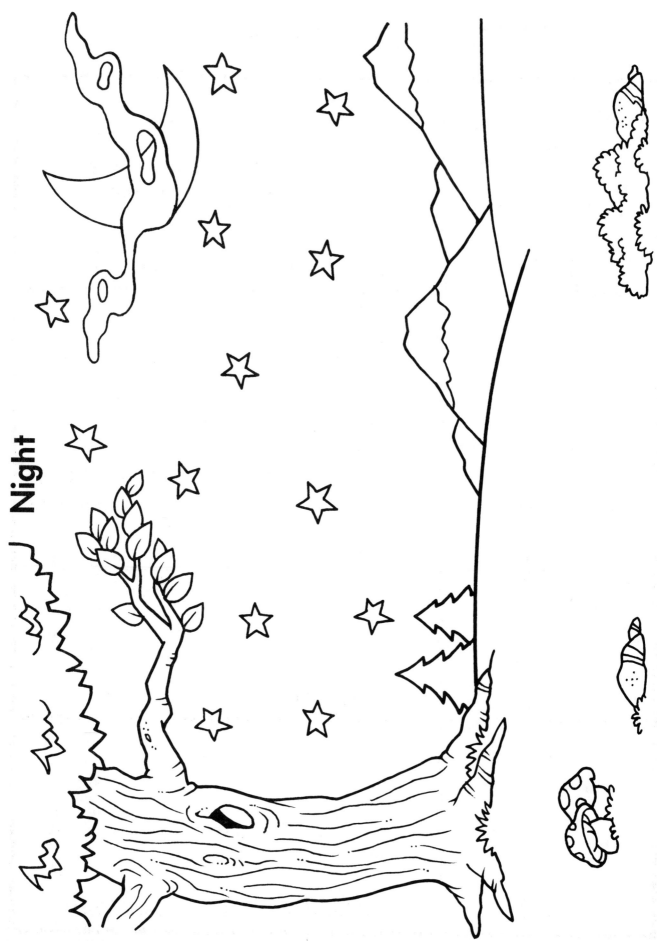

Night

Leap into Literacy • Fall © 2003 Creative Teaching Press

Animal Cards

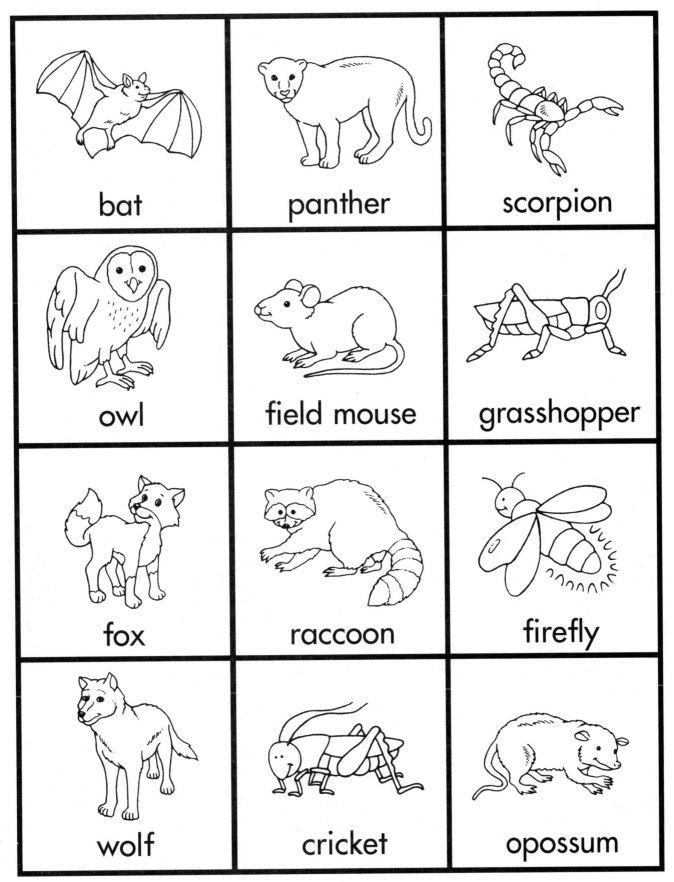

bat

panther

scorpion

owl

field mouse

grasshopper

fox

raccoon

firefly

wolf

cricket

opossum

Bats

Leap into Literacy • Fall © 2003 Creative Teaching Press

Cave

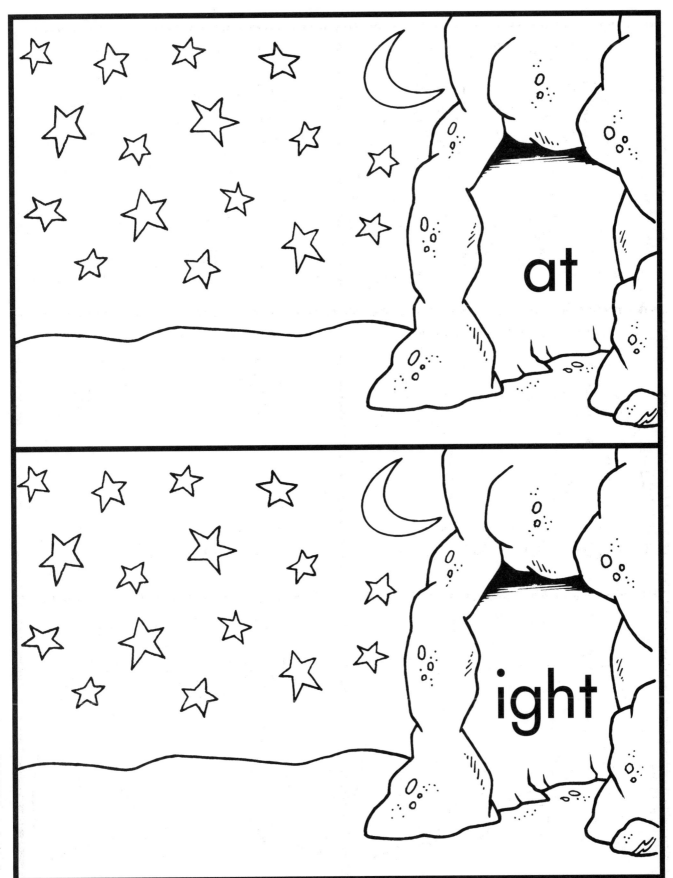

at

ight

Cave

ave

ark

Direction Cards

Fly like a

.

Run like a

.

Howl like a

.

Leap like a

.

Crawl like a

.

Chirp like a

.

Climb like a

.

Jump like a

.

Two Kinds of Pumpkins

(to the tune of "London Bridges Falling Down")

Some pumpkins are best to carve, best to carve, best to carve.
Some pumpkins are best to carve. They're big and soft inside.

Some pumpkins are best to eat, best to eat, best to eat.
Some pumpkins are best to eat. They're small and taste so good.

Pumpkins are picked in the fall, in the fall, in the fall.
Pumpkins are picked in the fall to carve or eat in pie!

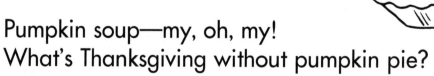

Pumpkin Goodies

Go pick a pumpkin and look in a book.
How many pumpkin foods can we cook?

Pumpkin bread and muffins, too—
Pumpkin seeds are good for you!

Pumpkin soup—my, oh, my!
What's Thanksgiving without pumpkin pie?

Pumpkin pudding and pumpkin cake—
How many pumpkin foods can you make?

Leap into Literacy • Fall © 2003 Creative Teaching Press

Two Kinds of Pumpkins

by _____

Some pumpkins are best to carve,
best to carve, best to carve.

1

Some pumpkins are best to carve.
They're big and soft inside.

2

Some pumpkins are best to eat,
best to eat, best to eat.

3

Leap into Literacy • Fall © 2003 Creative Teaching Press

Some pumpkins are best to eat.
They're small and taste so good.

4

Pumpkins are picked in the fall,
in the fall, in the fall.
Pumpkins are picked in the fall
to carve or eat in pie!

5

Leap into Literacy • Fall © 2003 Creative Teaching Press

Pumpkin Goodies

by _____

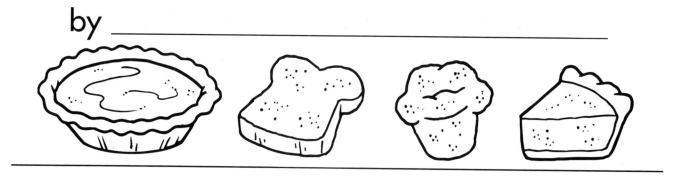

Go pick a pumpkin and look in a book.
How many pumpkin foods can we cook?

Leap into Literacy • Fall © 2003 Creative Teaching Press

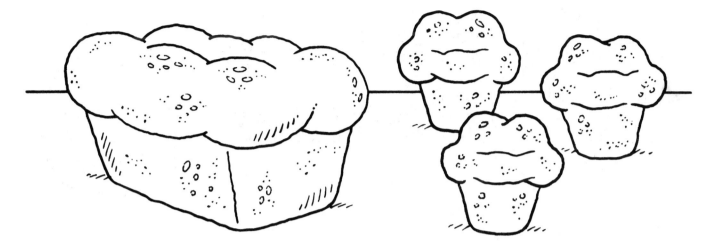

Pumpkin bread and muffins, too—
pumpkin seeds are good for you!

2

Pumpkin soup—my, oh, my!

3

What's Thanksgiving without pumpkin pie?

4

Pumpkin pudding and pumpkin cake—
how many pumpkin foods can you make?

5

Leap into Literacy • Fall © 2003 Creative Teaching Press

Find Out the Facts

Pumpkins

ACTIVITIES

Use the fun facts reproducible on page 76 and the activity suggestions on page 6 to introduce children to new vocabulary and extend their science knowledge.

Literature Links

Fiction

The Pumpkin Blanket
by Deborah Turney Zagwyn
(Ten Speed Press)

Pumpkin Jack
by Will Hubbell
(Albert Whitman)

Pumpkin Light
by David Ray
(Philomel)

The Pumpkin Runner
by Marsha Diane Arnold
(Dial Books for Young Readers)

Too Many Pumpkins
by Linda White
(Holiday House)

Nonfiction

It's Pumpkin Time
by Zoe Hall
(Scholastic)

The Pumpkin Book
by Gail Gibbons
(Holiday House)

Pumpkin Circle
by George Levenson
(Tricycle Press)

The Pumpkin Patch
by Elizabeth King
(Viking Penguin)

Pumpkins
by Ann L. Burckhardt
(Bridgestone Books)

Reading Log

Use the reproducible on page 77 as a reading log (see page 7).

Class Book

● Copy the class book reproducible (page 78) for children to complete.

● Have children draw what they would like to make with pumpkins.

Spring into Centers

A Match in the Patch

Skill: rhyming words

Materials

Vine reproducible (page 79)

Pumpkin Picture Cards (page 80)

crayons or markers

scissors

glue

Pumpkins

Make four copies of the Vine reproducible, and color them. Copy, color, and cut apart the Pumpkin Picture Cards. Glue the sock, train, bee, and pie picture cards to separate vines, and laminate the vines and cards. Ask children to choose a card and name the picture. Have children place the card on the vine with a rhyming picture. Tell children to place the remaining cards on vines. Then, encourage children to name the pictures on all the cards on each vine.

Seed Sort

Skill: recognizing number words

Pumpkins

Make three copies of the Pumpkins reproducible, and cut them apart. Write the number words for one to ten on separate pumpkins, and color and laminate them. Have children place the pumpkins on a flat surface in numerical order. Tell them to place the same number of seeds, beans, or cubes as the number word on each pumpkin. To simplify the activity, draw the number of dots that matches the number words on the pumpkins. Have children place a seed on each dot as they count aloud.

Materials

Pumpkins reproducible (page 81)

scissors

crayons or markers

pumpkin seeds, dried white beans, or linking cubes

Pumpkin Purchases

Skill: recognizing number words

Pumpkins

Make a class set of the Pick a Pumpkin reproducibles. Have children cut apart the strips and staple them together in numerical order. Help children write the missing number words on the blank lines, and read the book together. Invite children to color their books and read them to each other.

Materials

Pick a Pumpkin reproducibles (pages 82–83)

scissors

crayons or markers

Pumpkin Fun Facts

Pumpkins have five parts: the shell, flesh, pulp, seeds, and stem.

Pumpkin vines can grow as long as 30 feet (9.1 m).

Orange stock pumpkins are large and have soft insides. This makes them the best for carving.

Yellow cheese pumpkins are smaller in size and taste better. The smaller a pumpkin is, the better it tastes.

It takes 80 to 120 days for a seed to grow into a pumpkin. A pumpkin is ready if it is hard and has a hollow sound when tapped.

The biggest pumpkin was grown in New York in 1996. It weighed 1,061 pounds (481 kg). That is about as much as a small car!

Leap into Literacy • Fall © 2003 Creative Teaching Press

Reading Log

Name _____ Date _____

My favorite book about **pumpkins** was

_____

because _____

_____.

Color one book each time you read or listen to a story about pumpkins.

Name _____ Date _____

I would like to make

_____

with pumpkins.

Leap into Literacy • Fall © 2003 Creative Teaching Press

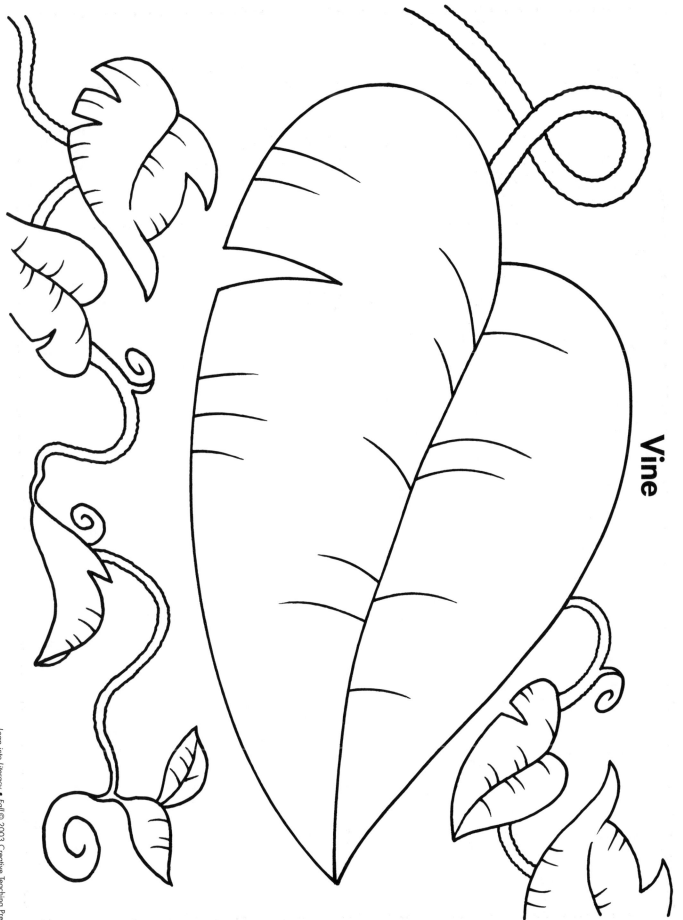

Vine

Pumpkin Picture Cards

Leap into Literacy • Fall © 2003 Creative Teaching Press

Pumpkins

 # Pick a Pumpkin

by _____

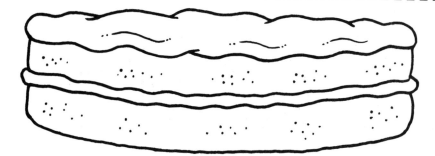

Pick a pumpkin—one, _____, three.
Make a cake and share it with me.

1

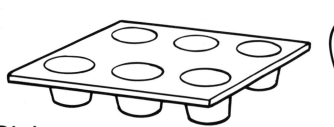

Pick another—_____, five, _____.
This one is for the muffin mix.

2

Pick a Pumpkin

Pick one more—seven, _____, nine.
On pie and pudding we will dine.

3

Pick the last—_____, eleven, twelve.
And put the cookbook back on the shelf.

4

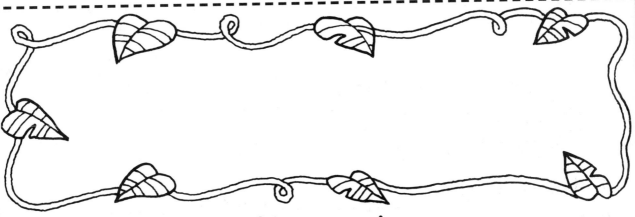

My favorite pumpkin treat is _____.

5

Crocs and Gators

(to the tune of "Old MacDonald Had a Farm")

Who has a long and narrow snout? Crocodiles do.
Who has bottom teeth sticking out? Crocodiles do.
They share their food with all their friends.
All day long they swim and swim.
Who makes you run when they come out? Crocodiles do!

Who has a broad and rounded snout? Alligators do.
Who has no bottom teeth sticking out? Alligators do.
They lay all day in the nice warm sun.
They care for their babies 'til they are only one.
Who makes you run when they come out? Alligators do!

Who has two sets of eyelids? Crocs and gators do.
Who guards their nest to protect their kids? Crocs and gators do.
Their teeth cannot be used to chew.
They swallow rocks to grind food through.
Who makes you run when they come out? Crocs and gators do!

Reptiles

Reptiles have backbones and a set of lungs.
Their mothers leave them when they are young.

All are covered with scales and shed their skin.
Their cold-blooded bodies match the temperature they're in.

They have no hair. Most hatch from eggs.
Some slither on the ground. Many have short legs.

They're cool and creepy and scaly, too.
It's fun to look at them in books or at the zoo!

Leap into Literacy • Fall © 2003 Creative Teaching Press

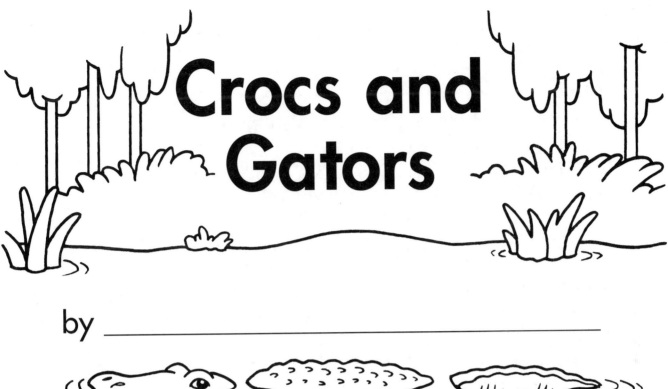

Crocs and Gators

by _____

Who has a long and narrow snout?
Crocodiles do.

Who has bottom teeth sticking out? Crocodiles do.
They share their food with all their friends.

2

All day long they swim and swim.
Who makes you run when they come out?
Crocodiles do!

3

Leap into Literacy • Fall © 2003 Creative Teaching Press

Who has a broad and rounded snout?
Alligators do.

4

Who has no bottom teeth sticking out?
Alligators do.
They lay all day in the nice warm sun.

5

Leap into Literacy • Fall © 2003 Creative Teaching Press

Reptiles 87

They care for their babies 'til they are only one.
Who makes you run when they come out?
Alligators do!

6

Who has two sets of eyelids?
Crocs and gators do.

7

Leap into Literacy • Fall © 2003 Creative Teaching Press

Who guards their nest to protect their kids?
Crocs and gators do.
Their teeth cannot be used to chew.

8

They swallow rocks to grind food through.
Who makes you run when they come out?
Crocs and gators do!

9

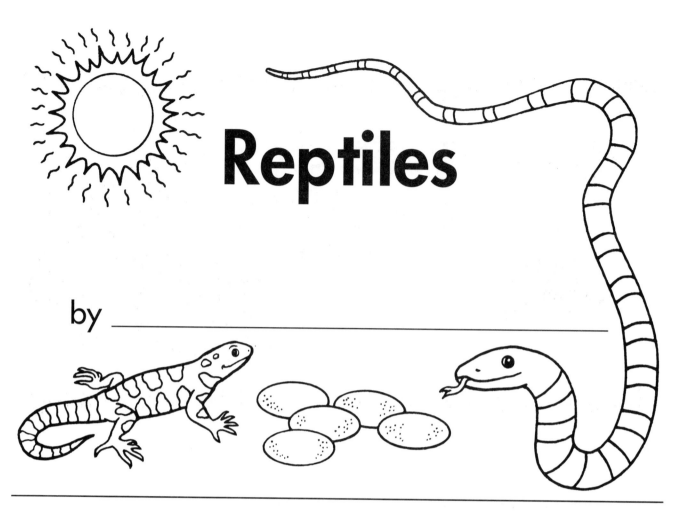

Reptiles

by _____

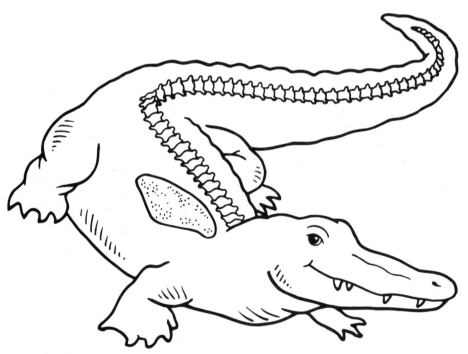

Reptiles have backbones and a set of lungs.

Leap into Literacy • Fall © 2003 Creative Teaching Press

Their mothers leave them when they are young.

2

All are covered with scales and shed their skin.

3

Leap into Literacy • Fall © 2003 Creative Teaching Press

Their cold-blooded bodies match
the temperature they're in.

4

They have no hair. Most hatch from eggs.

5

Leap into Literacy • Fall © 2003 Creative Teaching Press

Some slither on the ground. Many have short legs.

6

They're cool and creepy and scaly, too.
It's fun to look at them in books or at the zoo!

7

Leap into Literacy • Fall © 2003 Creative Teaching Press

Reptiles

ACTIVITIES

Find Out the Facts

Use the fun facts reproducible on page 97 and the activity suggestions on page 6 to introduce children to new vocabulary and extend their science knowledge.

Bounce into Books

Literature Links

Fiction

Alligator Baby
by Robert Munsch
(CARTWHEEL BOOKS®)

Lizard's Home
by George Shannon
(GREENWILLOW BOOKS)

Reptiles Are My Life
by Megan McDonald
(ORCHARD BOOKS)

The Selfish Crocodile
by Charles Faustin
(LITTLE TIGER PRESS)

Snake Alley Band
by Elizabeth Nygaard and Betsy Lewin
(BANTAM DOUBLEDAY DELL)

Nonfiction

Amazing Crocodiles and Reptiles
by Mary Ling
(ALFRED A. KNOPF BOOKS)

Eye Wonder: Reptiles
by Simon Holland
(DK PUBLISHING)

How to Hide a Crocodile and Other Reptiles
by Ruth Heller
(GROSSET & DUNLAP)

I Can Read About Reptiles
by David Cutts
(TROLL COMMUNICATIONS)

National Audubon Society First Field Guide: Reptiles
by John L. Behler
(SCHOLASTIC)

Reading Log

Use the reproducible on page 98 as a reading log (see page 7).

Class Book

- Copy the class book reproducible (page 99) for children to complete.
- Have children draw their favorite reptile and write about it.

Spring into Centers

Reptile Races

Skills: recognizing action verbs and following directions

Reptiles

Make an enlarged copy of the Reptile Racetrack reproducible, and color and laminate it. Copy, cut apart, and laminate the Game Cards, and place them facedown in a pile. Give each child a milk container cap and sticker (or write children's names on labels to place on the caps) to use as a game marker, and have children place their markers on "Start." Have children draw a card, and read aloud the directions with them. Tell children to move their game marker according to the directions on their card. Have them take turns drawing cards and moving their marker until each child reaches the end of the game board. If a child is unable to move to the place directed by a card, play passes to the next child.

Materials

Reptile Racetrack reproducible (page 100)

Game Cards (page 101)

crayons or markers

scissors

milk container caps

reptile stickers or circular labels

Listen to the Crocodiles

Skill: identifying beginning, middle, and ending sounds

Materials

Crocodiles reproducible
(page 102)
....
Crocodile Cards (page 103)
....
crayons or markers
....
scissors
....
pebble or penny

Reptiles

Copy, color, and cut apart the Crocodiles reproducible and the Crocodile Cards. Give each child a crocodile and a pebble (because crocodiles swallow rocks for digestion) or a penny, and tell children to place all of the crocodiles faceup on a flat surface. Invite children to choose a card and name the picture on it. Ask children to decide whether they hear the /c/ sound at the beginning, middle, or ending of the word. Have them place the pebble or penny on the crocodile's head if it is a beginning sound, on the back if it is a middle sound, or on the tail if it is an ending sound.

Silly Snakes

Skills: forming and recognizing letters

Materials

Letter Cards
(pages 104–106)
....
scissors
....
play dough

Reptiles

Copy, cut apart, and laminate the Letter Cards. Have children spread the cards faceup on a table. Give children pieces of play dough, and invite them to make a "snake" by rolling it on the table. Ask children to pick a letter card and say the name of the letter and the sound it makes. Then, have them use their snake to outline the letter on their card. To simplify the activity, make the play dough snakes for children prior to beginning the activity.

Reptile Fun Facts

Reptiles are the last living relatives of the dinosaurs.

Reptiles are sometimes called "living fossils" because they have been around for 240 million years.

Reptiles have backbones and lungs. All reptiles shed their skin and are covered with scales or bony plates.

Reptiles lay eggs.

Both alligators and crocodiles have a second set of eyelids that they use like goggles under the water.

Alligators' and crocodiles' teeth can only grab and tear food. They must swallow rocks to help crush the food they have eaten.

Leap into Literacy • Fall © 2003 Creative Teaching Press

Reading Log

Name _____ Date _____

My favorite book about **reptiles** was

_____

because _____

_____.

Color one book each time you read or listen to a story about reptiles.

Leap into Literacy • Fall © 2003 Creative Teaching Press

Name _____ Date _____

My favorite reptile is the

_____ because

_____ .

Leap into Literacy • Fall © 2003 Creative Teaching Press

Reptile Racetrack

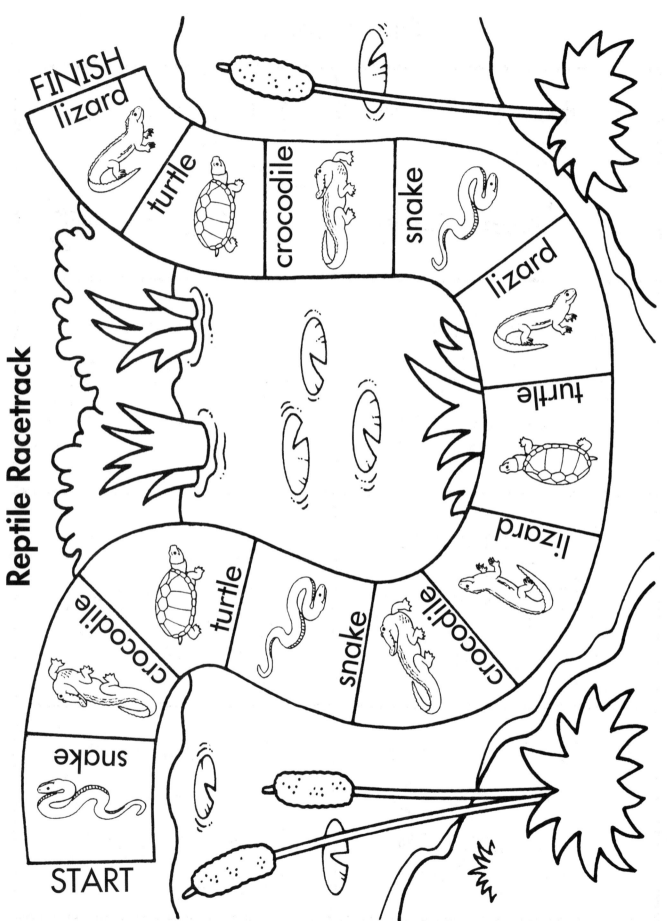

FINISH
lizard
turtle
crocodile
snake
lizard
turtle
lizard
crocodile
snake
turtle
crocodile
snake
START

Leap into Literacy • Fall © 2003 Creative Teaching Press

Game Cards

Slither to the next

Slither to the next

Crawl to the next

Crawl to the next

Swim to the next

Swim to the next

Run to the next

Run to the next

Crocodiles

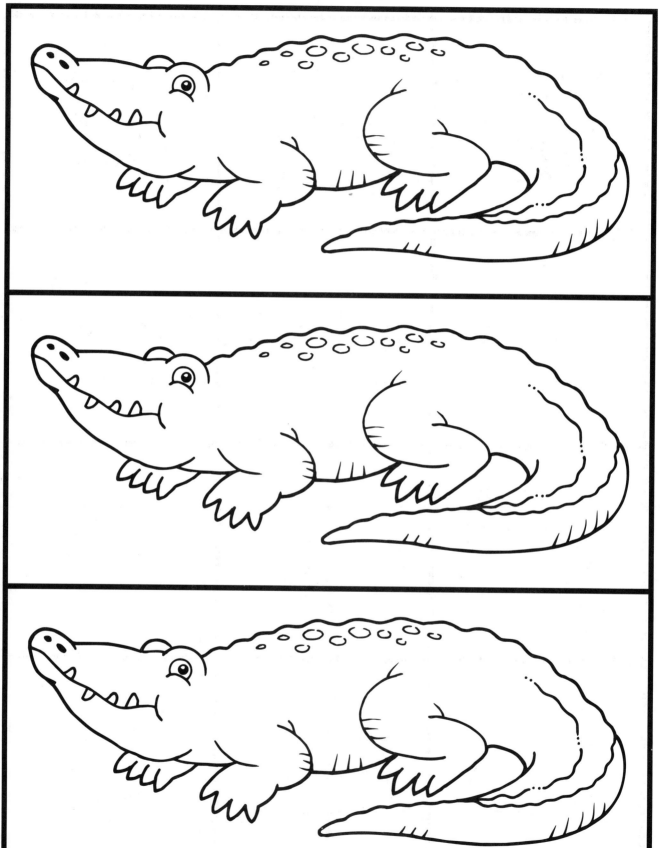

Leap into Literacy • Fall © 2003 Creative Teaching Press

Crocodile Cards

Letter Cards

A	B	C
D	E	F
G	H	I

Letter Cards

J	K	L
M	N	O
P	Q	R

Letter Cards

S	T	U
V	W	X
Y	Z	

Leap into Literacy • Fall © 2003 Creative Teaching Press

Taste

(to the tune of "Mary Had a Little Lamb")

What can you taste that is sour, that is sour, that is sour?
What can you taste that is sour?
A lemon—the color of gold.

What can you taste that is sweet, that is sweet, that is sweet?
What can you taste that is sweet?
An ice cream cake so cold.

What can you taste that is salty, that is salty, that is salty?
What can you taste that is salty?
Peanuts—crunchy and small.

What can you taste that is bitter, that is bitter, that is bitter?
What can you taste that is bitter?
Cranberries—round like a ball.

What a Treat!

Look with your eyes at the beautiful flower.
Smell with your nose the lemon so sour.
Hear with your ears the roar of the jet.
Feel with your skin the water so wet.
Taste with your tongue the cupcake so sweet.
Using your senses is really a treat!

Taste

by _____

What can you taste that is sour,
that is sour, that is sour?
What can you taste that is sour?
A lemon—the color of gold.

1

Leap into Literacy • Fall © 2003 Creative Teaching Press

What can you taste that is sweet,
that is sweet, that is sweet?

2

What can you taste that is sweet?
An ice cream cake so cold.

3

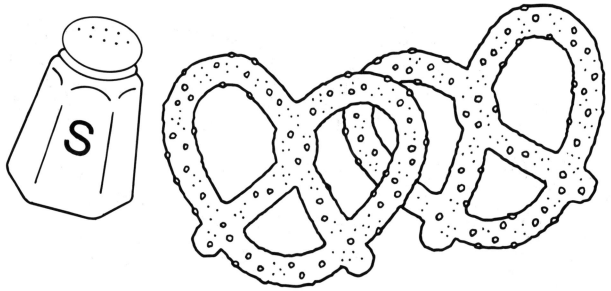

What can you taste that is salty,
that is salty, that is salty?

4

What can you taste that is salty?
Peanuts—crunchy and small.

Leap into Literacy • Fall © 2003 Creative Teaching Press

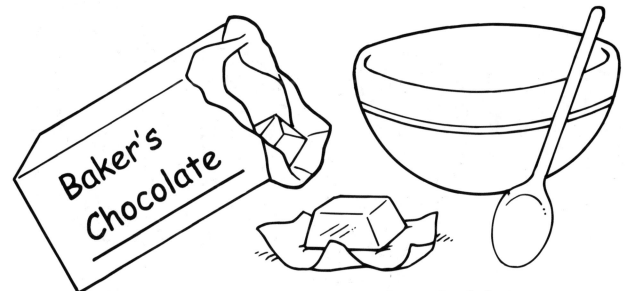

What can you taste that is bitter,
that is bitter, that is bitter?

6

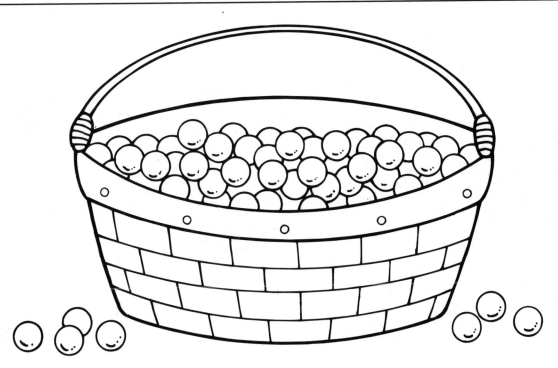

What can you taste that is bitter?
Cranberries—round like a ball.

What a Treat!

by _____

Look with your eyes at the beautiful flower.

1

Leap into Literacy • Fall © 2003 Creative Teaching Press

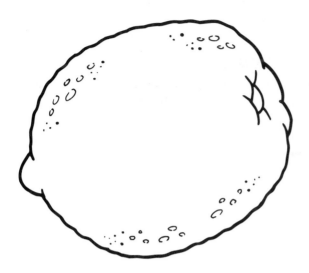

Smell with your nose the lemon so sour.

2

Hear with your ears the roar of the jet.

3

Feel with your skin the water so wet.

4

Taste with your tongue the cupcake so sweet.
Using your senses is really a treat!

5

Leap into Literacy • Fall © 2003 Creative Teaching Press

Find Out the Facts

Senses

ACTIVITIES

Use the fun facts reproducible on page 118 and the

activity suggestions on page 6 to introduce children to

new vocabulary and extend their science knowledge.

Bounce into Books

Literature Links

Fiction

Brown Bear, Brown Bear, What Do You See?
by Bill Martin Jr. and Eric Carle
(HENRY HOLT AND COMPANY)

Little Bunny Follows His Nose
by Katherine Howard
(GOLDEN BOOKS)

Polar Bear, Polar Bear, What Do You Hear?
by Bill Martin Jr. and Eric Carle
(HENRY HOLT AND COMPANY)

What Do You See When You Shut Your Eyes?
by Cynthia Zarin
(HOUGHTON MIFFLIN)

Why Butterflies Go by on Silent Wings
by Marguerite W. Davol
(SCHOLASTIC)

Nonfiction

How Do We Taste and Smell?
by Carol Ballard
(STECK-VAUGHN COMPANY)

Look At Your Body: Senses
by Steve Parker
(MILLBROOK PRESS)

My Five Senses
by Aliki Brandenberg
(HARPERTROPHY)

My Five Senses
by Margaret Miller
(SIMON & SCHUSTER)

You Can't Smell a Flower with Your Ear!
by Joanna Cole
(GROSSET & DUNLAP)

Reading Log

Use the reproducible on page 119 as a reading log (see page 7).

Class Book

● Copy the class book reproducible (page 120) for children to complete.

● Have children draw an object they can explore with their senses and write about it.

Spring into Centers

"Orange" You Glad?

Skill: story sequencing

Materials

Sense Sequence reproducible (page 121)

crayons or markers

scissors

Senses

Copy, color, and cut apart the Sense Sequence reproducible. Write one letter (i.e., *a, b, c, d, e, f*) on the back of each card in alphabetical order to show the correct sequence of the cards. Have children shuffle the cards and place them faceup on a flat surface. Ask children to examine the scene on each card and arrange the cards to "tell" a story. Then, invite children to turn over the cards to verify that the letters on the back of the cards are in alphabetical order. To simplify the activity, place the cards facedown in alphabetical order. Have children turn over one card at a time to see the correct story sequence.

Opposite Point of View

Skill: following directions

 Copy, color, cut apart, and laminate the Glasses reproducible and Opposite Cards. Give each child a pair of glasses, and scatter the cards faceup on a flat surface. Ask children to find a pair of opposite cards and place one on each lens of their glasses. Invite children to describe their pairs of opposites to each other.

Materials

Glasses reproducible (page 122)

Opposite Cards (page 123)

crayons or markers

scissors

Three Cheers for Chewing!

Skill: recognizing consonant digraphs

 Give each child a copy of the Table and Chair reproducible and Words to Chew On Cards. Tell children to color and cut apart their cards. Ask children to name the words on their cards and insert them in the frame *I sit in my chair and chew _____*. Have children choose their favorite food card and glue it on their reproducible. Invite children to write the name of the food in the frame at the top of their paper and draw themselves sitting in the chair. Bind children's papers together in a class book titled *Three Cheers for Chewing!*

Materials

Table and Chair reproducible (page 124)

Words to Chew On Cards (page 125)

crayons or colored pencils

scissors

glue

bookbinding materials

Senses Fun Facts

There are five main senses: hearing, sight, smell, taste, and touch.

There are also other senses that give information about the body such as balance, hunger, pain, and thirst.

There are about 10,000 taste buds on our tongue. They allow us to taste bitter, sweet, salty, and sour.

When light is bright, our pupils grow small. This keeps too much light from hurting our eyes.

More than half of the information that goes to our brain comes through our eyes.

Many animals, including bats, whales, and dogs, can hear sounds far past a human's range of hearing.

Leap into Literacy • Fall © 2003 Creative Teaching Press

Reading Log

Name _____ Date _____

My favorite book about **senses** was

_____

because _____

_____.

Color one book each time you read or listen to a story about senses.

Name _____ Date _____

 You can _____

a _____.

Leap into Literacy • Fall © 2003 Creative Teaching Press

Sense Sequence

Glasses

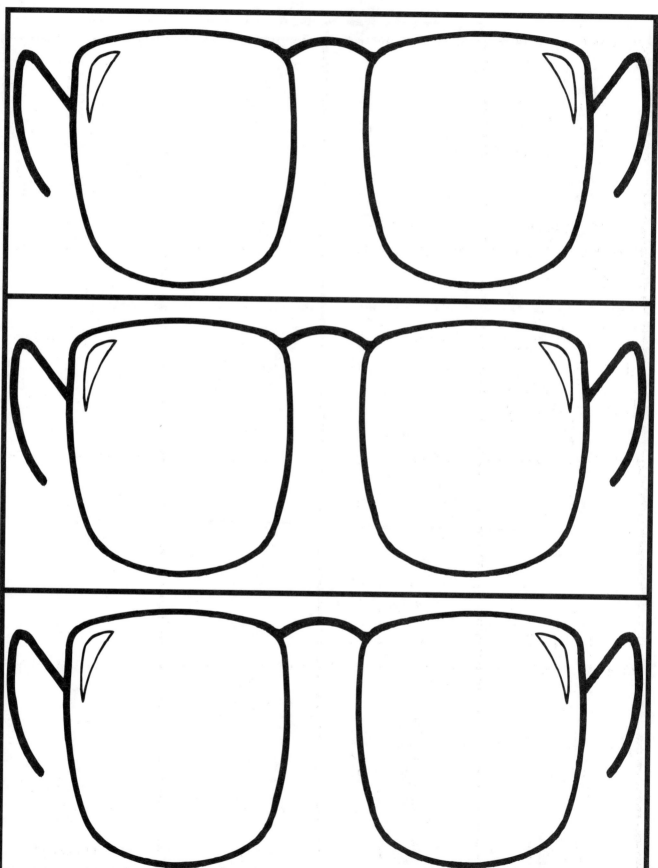

Leap into Literacy • Fall © 2003 Creative Teaching Press

Opposite Cards

happy	sad	wet	dry
in	out	up	down
night	day	hot	cold
short	tall	top	bottom

Table and Chair

I sit in my chair and chew

Chomp! Chomp!

Words to Chew On Cards

cheese

chicken

chips

chocolate

chili

chestnuts

chewing gum

cherries

What Do People Think of Spiders?

(to the tune of "Row, Row, Row Your Boat")

What do people think of spiders—
Scary or poisonous,
Ugly, creepy, crawly,
Or very dangerous?

Wait! Spiders can be our friends.
Harmful bugs they eat.
So please be nice to spiders.
Their help just can't be beat.

Eight

How many legs does a spider have?
Eight creeping legs with fur.

How many eyes does a spider have?
Eight dark eyes, yes, sir.

Count them—one, two, three. That's great!
Four, five, six, seven, and eight.

Eight eyes, eight legs—but not eight hearts.
What would you do will all those parts?

What Do People Think of Spiders?

by _____

What do people think of spiders—
scary or poisonous,

1

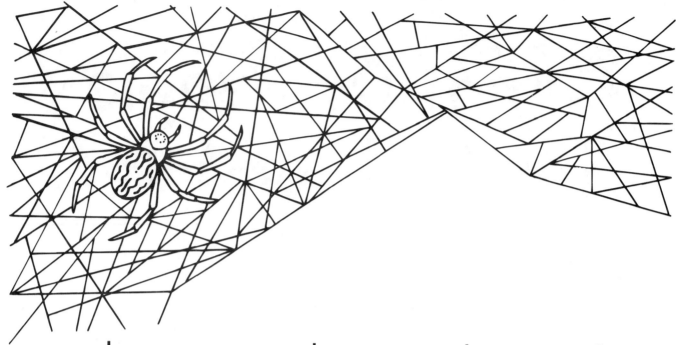

ugly, creepy, crawly, or very dangerous?

2

Wait! Spiders can be our friends.

Harmful bugs they eat.

4

So please be nice to spiders.
Their help just can't be beat.

Eight

by _____

How many legs does a spider have?
Eight creeping legs with fur.

Leap into Literacy • Fall © 2003 Creative Teaching Press

How many eyes does a spider have?
Eight dark eyes, yes, sir.

2

Count them—one, two, three. That's great!
Four, five, six, seven, and eight.

3

Eight eyes, eight legs—but not eight hearts.

4

What would you do will all those parts?

5

Leap into Literacy • Fall © 2003 Creative Teaching Press

Find Out the Facts

Use the fun facts reproducible on page 136 and the activity suggestions on page 6 to introduce children to new vocabulary and extend their science knowledge.

Bounce into Books

Literature Links

Fiction

Be Nice to Spiders
by Margaret Bloy Graham
(HARPERCOLLINS)

Dream Weaver
by Jonathan London
(SILVER WHISTLE)

Miss Spider's Tea Party
by David Kirk
(SCHOLASTIC)

Spiders Spin Webs
by Yvonne Winer
(CHARLESBRIDGE PUBLISHING)

The Very Busy Spider
by Eric Carle
(PHILOMEL)

Nonfiction

Amazing Spiders
by Alexandra Parsons
(ALFRED A. KNOPF BOOKS)

Eight Legs
by Dorothy M. Souza
(LERNER PUBLISHING)

Spiders
by Gail Gibbons
(HOLIDAY HOUSE)

Spiders and Their Web Sites
by Margery Facklam
(LITTLE, BROWN & COMPANY)

Spiders Are Not Insects
by Allan Fowler
(CHILDREN'S PRESS)

Reading Log

Use the reproducible on page 137 as a reading log (see page 7).

Class Book

● Copy the class book reproducible (page 138) for children to complete.

● Have children draw what they would do if they had eight legs like a spider and write about it.

Spring into Centers

Web Words

Skill: recognizing word family words

Materials

Web reproducible (page 139)

Flies reproducible (page 140)

crayons or markers

scissors

Spiders

Copy and color the Web reproducible, and laminate it. Copy and cut apart the Flies reproducible. Write *cry, my, by, try, spy, why, to, and, we, it, me,* and *the* on separate flies, and laminate them. Scatter the flies faceup around the web. Invite children to pick a fly and read the word on it. Have children place the fly on the web if the word rhymes with *fly.*

Eight Little Spiders Hanging from a Gate

Skill: rhythm and rhyme

 Copy a class set of the Spiders on a Gate reproducible. Ask children to color their paper and cut apart the gate pieces. Tell children to tape together the pieces to form one long gate. Show children how to cut along the dotted lines to make eight flaps. Write the following rhyme on chart paper, and teach it to the children.

Eight little spiders hanging from a gate.
The first one said, "Oh, my! It's getting late.
I must get home—I just can't wait!"
Now there are seven spiders hanging from a gate.

Have children fold back spider number 8. Count the number of spiders that remain. Change the boldfaced words to *seven*, repeat the verse, and have children fold back spider number 7. Have children repeat the process with six to zero.

Materials

Spiders on a Gate reproducible (page 141)
.....
crayons or markers
.....
scissors
.....
tape
.....
chart paper

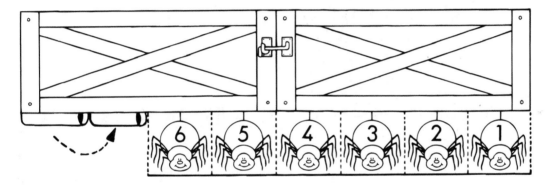

I Spy a Spider

Skill: identifying opposites

 Create an I Spy a Spider mini-book for each child. Copy the I Spy a Spider reproducibles, cut them apart, place them in order, and staple them down the left-hand side. Give each child a mini-book. Read aloud page 1 with children, and ask them to use the sentence to help them decide where a spider should be placed. For example on page 1, children would place a spider climbing *up* the wall. Invite children to press their thumb on an inkpad and then on the corresponding place on their page. Have children draw four legs on each side of the thumbprint and add facial features to make a "spider." Repeat these steps for pages 2 to 6. Then, read aloud the sentence on page 7 with children, and have them create a spider anywhere on the page and add background scenery. Ask children to say a sentence about where their spider is playing and color the pages in their mini-book. Encourage children to read the mini-book when they are finished.

Materials

I Spy a Spider reproducibles (pages 142–143)
.....
scissors
.....
inkpad
.....
crayons or markers

Spider Fun Facts

A spider's body has two parts. All spiders have eight legs and most have eight eyes.

When a spider grows too big for its hard, outer skin, it sheds its skin. This is called molting.

All spiders make silk from their bodies. Some build webs to catch insects for food.

There are different types of webs, including the funnel, orb, tangle, and triangle.

Spiders are covered in oil so they will not stick to their silky webs like insects do.

Spiders are helpful because they eat many insects that are dangerous to us and the food we grow.

Reading Log

Name _____ Date _____

My favorite book about **spiders** was

_____

because _____

_____.

Color one book each time you read or listen to a story about spiders.

Leap into Literacy • Fall © 2003 Creative Teaching Press

Name _____ Date _____

If I had eight legs like a spider,

I would _____

_____ .

Leap into Literacy • Fall © 2003 Creative Teaching Press

Web

Flies

Leap into Literacy • Fall © 2003 Creative Teaching Press

Spiders on a Gate

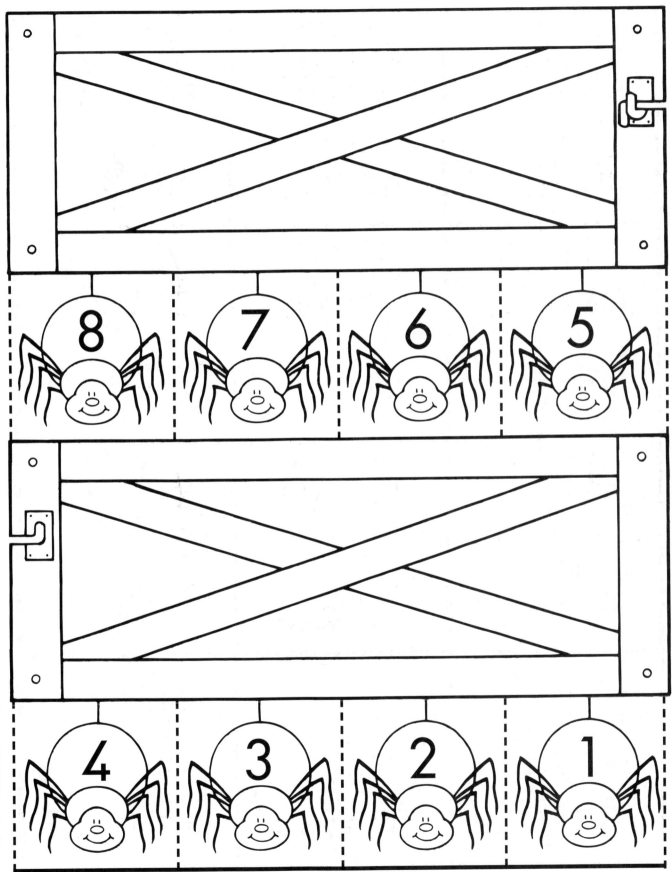

I Spy a Spider

by _____

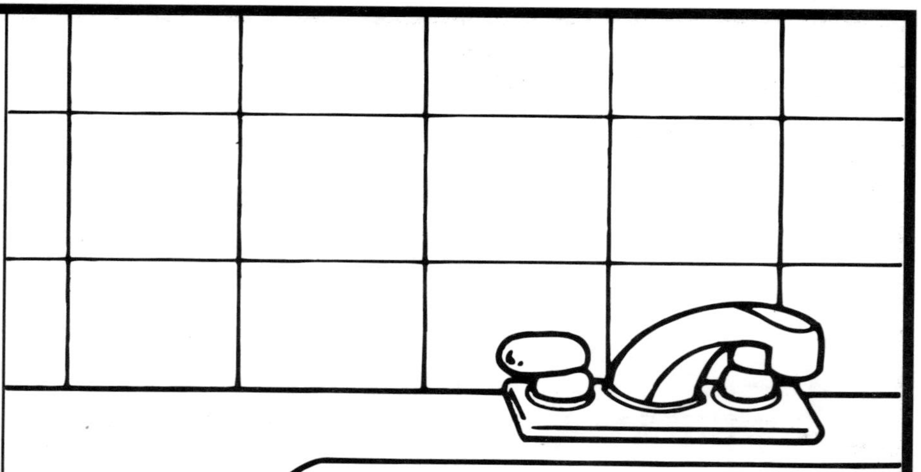

I spy a spider climbing **up** a wall.

1

I spy a spider crawling **over** a ball.

2

I spy a spider sneaking **under** a chair.

3

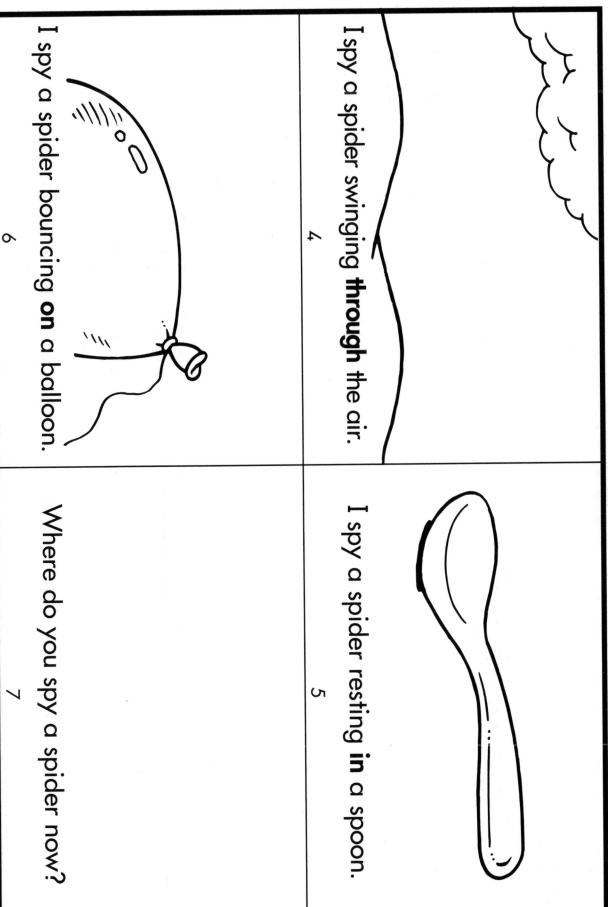

I spy a spider swinging **through** the air.

4

I spy a spider resting **in** a spoon.

5

I spy a spider bouncing **on** a balloon.

6

Where do you spy a spider now?

7

Fruitful Trees

(to the tune of "Pop Goes the Weasel")

We like to eat the fruits of trees,
Like apples and bananas,
Oranges, cherries, pears, and plums.
Oh! So delicious!

Nuts also come from trees,
Like hazelnuts and almonds,
Walnuts, chestnuts, and pecans.
Crack! Break them open!

Terrific Trees

Trees have many uses.
They give oxygen to living things.
And those big sturdy branches
Can hold little babies' swings.

Paper and pencils come from trees.
They are made from the wood.
Do you like maple syrup and bubble gum?
A tree's sap makes them taste so good!

Leap into Literacy • Fall © 2003 Creative Teaching Press

Fruitful Trees

by _____

We like to eat the fruits of trees,

1

like apples and bananas,

2

oranges, cherries, pears, and plums.

3

Leap into Literacy • Fall © 2003 Creative Teaching Press

Oh! So delicious!

4

Nuts also come from trees,

like hazelnuts and almonds,

6

walnuts, chestnuts, and pecans.
Crack! Break them open!

Leap into Literacy • *Fall* © 2003 Creative Teaching Press

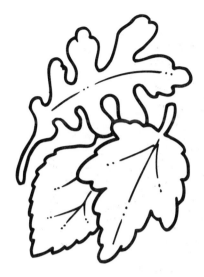

Terrific Trees

by _____

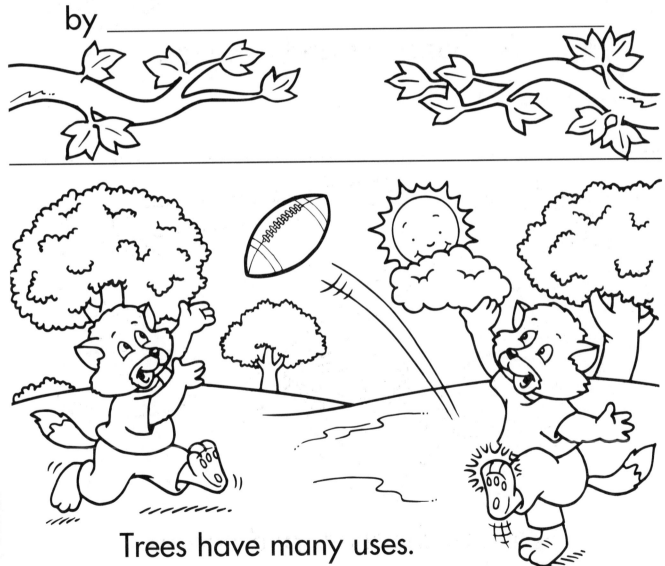

Trees have many uses.
They give oxygen to living things.

And those big sturdy branches
can hold little babies' swings.

2

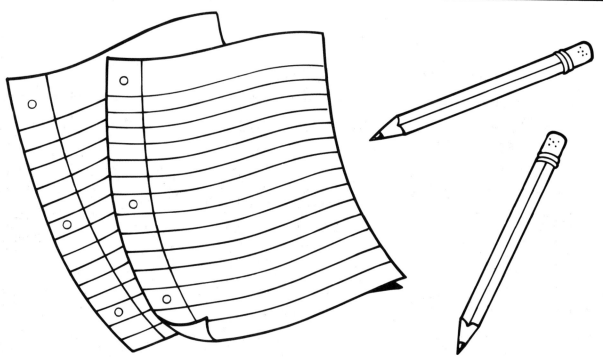

Paper and pencils come from trees.
They are made from the wood.

3

Leap into Literacy • Fall © 2003 Creative Teaching Press

Do you like maple syrup and bubble gum?

4

A tree's sap makes them taste so good!

Trees

ACTIVITIES

Find Out the Facts

Use the fun facts reproducible on page 155 and the activity suggestions on page 6 to introduce children to new vocabulary and extend their science knowledge.

Bounce into Books

Literature Links

Fiction

Apple Tree
by Peter Parnall
(ATHENEUM)

The Giving Tree
by Shel Silverstein
(HARPERCOLLINS)

Mary Margaret's Tree
by Blair Drawson
(ORCHARD BOOKS)

The Sugaring-Off Party
by Jonathan London
(DUTTON)

Tree Is Nice
by Janice May Udry
(HARPERCOLLINS)

Nonfiction

Be a Friend to Trees
by Patricia Lauber
(HARPERCOLLINS)

Crinkleroot's Guide to Knowing the Trees
by Jim Arnosky
(SIMON & SCHUSTER)

Redwoods Are the Tallest Trees in the World
by David Adler
(HARPERCOLLINS)

A Tree Is a Home
by Alden Kelley
(CREATIVE TEACHING PRESS)

A Tree Is Growing
by Arthur Dorros
(SCHOLASTIC)

Reading Log

Use the reproducible on page 156 as a reading log (see page 7).

Class Book

● Copy the class book reproducible (page 157) for children to complete.

● Have children draw a picture of something made from wood and write about it.

Nutty Words

Skill: identifying middle and ending sounds

Trees

Make a copy of the Basket reproducible, and write *Nutty Words* along the bottom. Make a class set of the revised paper and the Nutty Word Cards. Give each child a basket and a set of cards. Tell children to color and cut out their basket and glue it to a piece of construction paper. Ask children to say *nutty* and emphasize the *-ut* sound in the word. Have them cut apart their cards, use a brown marker or crayon to circle the letters "ut" in each word, and glue the cards in or around their basket. Encourage children to read their words to each other.

Materials

Basket reproducible (page 24)

Nutty Word Cards (page 158)

scissors

crayons or markers

glue

construction paper

brown marker or crayon

Fruit between Friends

Skill: discriminating between singular and plural words

Materials

One for Me reproducible (page 159)

Fruit Cards (page 160)

crayons or markers

scissors

glue

Trees

Make a class set of the One for Me reproducible and the Fruit Cards. Have children color and cut apart their cards. Ask them to choose a fruit they like, glue it in the first bowl, and write its name in the first blank. Tell children to glue the card that shows two pieces of the same fruit in the second bowl and write its name in the second blank. Encourage children to identify the difference between the singular and plural form of the same word.

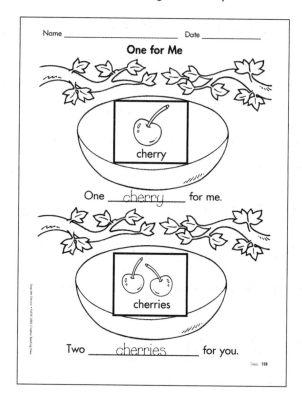

ABC Tree

Skill: recognizing color words

Materials

Tree reproducible (page 25)

Fruit Cards (page 160)

colored paper (yellow, orange, red, green, and purple)

scissors

crayons or markers

Trees

Copy the Tree reproducible on yellow, orange, red, green, and purple paper, write the name of the colors on the trees, and laminate them. Copy and cut apart the Fruit Cards. Color the banana yellow, the orange orange, the cherry red, the pear green, and the plum purple, and laminate the cards. Place the trees on a flat surface and the cards faceup below them. Place the plum on the purple tree, and say *Can you see the **purple plum** on the **purple** tree?* Invite children to take turns placing pieces of fruit on the coordinating trees and changing the color words and the name of the fruit in the sentence frame.

Tree Fun Facts

Trees are important to all living things. They give off oxygen, which living things need to breathe.

Tree roots grow into the ground and hold a tree in place. Water from the ground goes into the roots and up to the tree.

Some tree leaves stop making sugar during the fall. The leaves lose their green color, so we see their other colors, like red, orange, and brown.

The wood from trees is used to make many things like paper, pencils, and houses.

Sap from different types of trees is used to make maple syrup, chewing gum, soap, and rubber.

Redwoods are the tallest trees in the world and can be found in California and Oregon.

Reading Log

Name _____ Date _____

My favorite book about **trees** was _____

_____

because _____

_____.

Color one book each time you read or listen to a story about trees.

Leap into Literacy • Fall © 2003 Creative Teaching Press

Name _____ Date _____

Wood comes from trees. Wood is

used to make_____

_____.

Nutty Word Cards

nut

cut

butterfly

coconut

button

butter

hut

shutter

One for Me

One _____ for me.

Two _____ for you.

Fruit Cards

banana	bananas
orange	oranges
cherry	cherries
pear	pears
plum	plums

Leap into Literacy • Fall © 2003 Creative Teaching Press